Things
to Make
and Do

Things
to Make
and Do
(and ways to make money too)

by LINDA BEECH

Illustrated by Ethel Gold

SCHOLASTIC BOOK SERVICES
NEW YORK · TORONTO · LONDON · AUCKLAND · SYDNEY · TOKYO

For Christopher
with sunshine and love

Copyright © 1972 by Linda Beech. All rights reserved. Published by Scholastic Book Services, a division of Scholastic Magazines, Inc.

18 17 16 15 14 13 12   7 8 9/7 01/8
Printed in the U.S.A.

Do Your Own Thing

This book is all about making things from stuff around the house, and having a good time doing it. It's also about earning a little money. A special section at the end of the book gives you important tips for making money — and for setting up your own business.

You'll find ideas here for things to make for holidays and for any day. The projects in this book are really just to start you off. You'll find you have many *more* ideas of your own. And you'll discover that doing your own thing is a lot more fun — and less expensive — than buying things in a store.

Tip to the wise: Whenever you need to use sharp instruments or fire, *have the permission and the help of a grown-up.* And wear old clothes, a smock, or a big apron while you work.

CONTENTS

PART I
THINGS TO MAKE

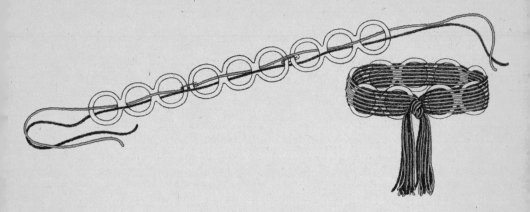

Where You Work:

Your work space can be the floor of your own room
or a family room. Or it may be the dining room table,
your desk, or a card table. Wherever it is, you'll want
to spread a plastic sheet and several layers of newspapers on top of your work surface, to protect it from
stains and scratches.

Your Supplies:

You'll find it helps not to have to go around collect-
ing materials each time you start to make something.

For storing supplies you'll need a large box, sometimes called a boodle box. You can make your own
boodle box out of a carton (*see page 12*).

In your boodle box keep a shoe box for storing pencils, Magic Markers, erasers, crayons, chalk, glue
(tightly capped), a ruler, a can opener, a hole puncher,
scissors, small rags, and a small box for pins, needles,

and buttons. There will still be room left in your boodle box for scraps of cloth, ribbon, threads, spools, cardboard, tracing paper, colored construction paper, graph paper, and a roll of shelf or contact paper.

Tips:

Read all directions through carefully before you start. Keep scissors, can opener, and other sharp tools out of the reach of your small brothers or sisters.

Scissors — Always cut *away* from you, and keep your eyes on what you're cutting. Don't try to cut heavy cardboard with scissors. Ask a grown-up to help with this kind of cutting.

Pencils — Keep sharpened. There are pencils with soft leads, best for making dark lines. Hard-lead pencils are best to use when you want a very light line. If you want to make "carbon paper," use the *side* of

your *soft* pencil point, and rub it over a piece of tracing paper. Then, to make copies of your design, place your "carbon paper" pencil-side down on a fresh piece of drawing paper. Place the design that you have drawn on tracing paper on top of the "carbon paper." Now use a *hard* pencil and trace the outline. Your design will be transferred.

Crayons — Experiment with your crayons. You can make a broader stroke by using the sides. Try painting over crayon marks for special effects. Experiment with different techniques. Other materials you might use are pastels (colored chalk), colored pencils, Cray Pas (oil base crayons), felt tipped pens (in washable colors), or pen and ink.

Food Containers — Be sure to wash thoroughly before storing.

Glues and Paints — Before using either, study the section at the very back of this book (*page 76*).

BOODLE BOX or CHILD'S TOY CHEST

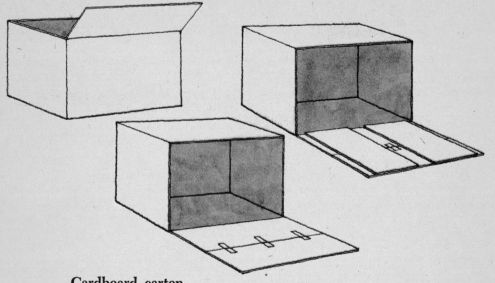

Cardboard carton
Contact paper or paper to be glued
Scissors
Glue
Cutouts or paints

Note: Your carton should be at least 16 inches long and 12 inches wide. You can use contact paper, or glue-smeared gift-wrap paper, wallpaper, or shelf paper. Use cutouts or paints for making decorative designs if you use plain paper.

1. Ask an adult to cut off all but one long flap.

2. Now turn the box on its side, open side facing you, and long *attached* flap extending flat on the floor. Place the long *cut* flap evenly beside it, and join the two long flaps with strips of tape.

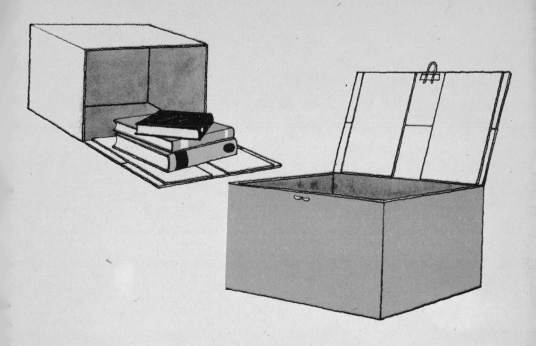

3. Now smear the short flaps with glue and place them, glue side down, on top of the long flaps. Press down firmly, and use heavy books to weigh down glued flaps until they have dried.

4. To cover the box, use the outside surfaces of the box for a pattern. Mark the paper to the shape of each side, then mark an extra ½ inch along each edge. This will give you an overlap for fold-overs along each edge of the box. Press the contact or glue-smeared paper on one side at a time, smoothing down fold-overs as you go.

5. To fasten the lid, glue and tape a loop of string to the open cover's edge. After covering (4) push a notebook fastener (*see drawing*) into the upper side of the box and open the "wings." You now have a lid that will stay shut.

POCKET SHELF

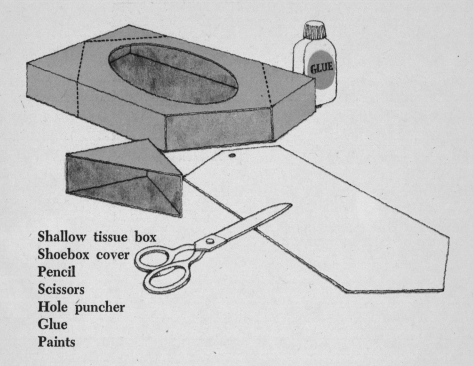

Shallow tissue box
Shoebox cover
Pencil
Scissors
Hole puncher
Glue
Paints

1. With a pencil, mark off triangles in four corners of
   tissue box — top, bottom, and sides. They will be
   equal triangles, half the width of the narrow end of
   the box (about 2⅜ inches) and 1¾ inches deep (the
   depth of the tissue box). The wide mouth of each
   triangle "pocket" will be 3⅜ inches.

2. Now cut out the pockets, starting from open top side
   of box. Each pocket should look like this:

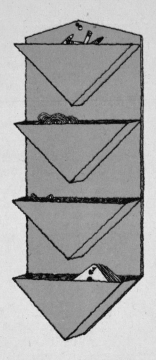

3. Break edges off shoe box cover and measure off and cut 3⅜-inch strip. Measure down an inch on each side and draw lines to top center of strip. Cut on lines. Punch a hole about ½ inch from top point.

4. Hold a pocket against bottom of inside of strip, trace triangular shape, and cut bottom of strip. Glue the back of the pocket to this shape. Glue a second pocket about ¾ inch down from hole. Now arrange other two pockets at equal distances, trace triangular shapes, and glue pockets in place. Press back of each pocket down firmly and let dry.

5. If desired, you can paint your pocket shelf. These pockets are handy for odds and ends — bobby pins, small jewelry, paper clips, rubber bands, etc.

BELT HANGER

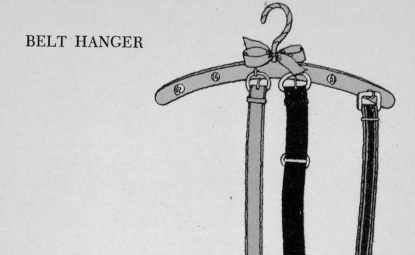

Flat-surface wooden coat hanger
Cup hooks (6)
Ribbon
Enamel paint
Ruler

1. Paint the wooden part of the hanger. Allow it to dry.

2. Next, measure off 6 places on the flat side of the hanger by making 3 pencil dots on either side of the hanger hook, an equal distance apart.

3. Lay the hanger flat, and screw the 6 cup hooks, evenly spaced, into the dots. (You may find it easier to screw in the cup hooks if you make a small starter hole first; this can be done by pounding a small nail, such as a flat-head nail, a little way into the wood.)

4. You can wind the hanger hook with ribbon or tie it with a perky bow.

JEWELRY TREE

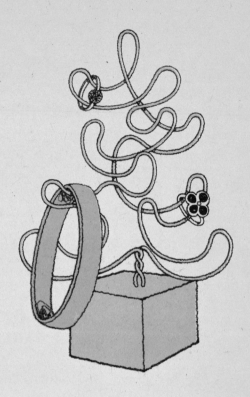

Rigid plastic foam, 3-inch cube
Plastic-covered bell wire, 3 feet

1. Bring the two ends of the wire together, and twist to make a short tree trunk.

2. Now, bend branches out on one side, then the other, twisting wire around to hold the branches and make the trunk rigid. Your tree can have a free form, with small triple branches at the top. Larger branches should be at the bottom.

3. Now, stick both ends of the wire into the plastic cube. If you wish, use latex paint to decorate the base. Your tree is now ready to hold its jewels.

GIFT TAGS

Used greeting cards
Scissors
Thread or thin string
Hole puncher

1. Look over greeting cards you have received. Select pictures or designs or greetings that would make attractive gift tags. *Be sure there is no writing on the back.* You can cut your tags into different shapes and sizes — triangles, squares, thin rectangles, circles, or make small folders.

2. Punch a hole in the corner of each tag. Then, take a 5-inch piece of thin string, fold in half, push the loop through the hole, then put both string ends through the loop and pull.

3. You can make gift tags for any occasion. Make up a box of them ahead of time. Or, you can make up packets of 10 gift tags and put them in plastic bags to sell.

PAPERWEIGHT STONES

Stones
Enamel paint
Clear shellac (thinned)

NOTE: Use several smooth, medium-sized stones; small jars of enamel paint can be bought in novelty stores; shellac is thinned with alcohol.

1. Wash stones and let them dry overnight. Then sketch simple designs in pencil on one side. You can practice your design or picture on paper before you sketch it on the stone.

2. Carefully paint your designs in bold colors. Again, allow the stone to dry overnight, then apply shellac with a brush.

3. Painted stones make handsome paperweights or table decorations.

FLOWER POT

16-ounce coffee can (used)
Brightly colored oilcloth, plastic cloth, or
   contact paper
Strong white glue
Scissors
Tape measure

1. Rinse out and dry the can. Using a nail, pound three (small) holes in the bottom.

2. Measure the height of the can from rim to rim and write it down. Now measure the distance around the can, add an extra ½ inch for overlap, and write down that measurement also. Now mark your material and cut out the piece you will use.

3. Spread the "wrong" side of the piece with glue, especially along the edges, if not using contact paper. Put down one edge of the sticky side along the seam of the can and pull the piece firmly around the

can until it overlaps. Press it down with your hands along the sides and seam.

4. Pour enough pebbles into the can to cover the bottom, then fill *halfway* with soil.

5. Hold your plant so that the roots rest gently on this soil, then sift more soil to within one inch of the top. Press soil down gently, and water. Set your potted plant on a saucer. Watch it grow!

BEAN BAG MITTEN

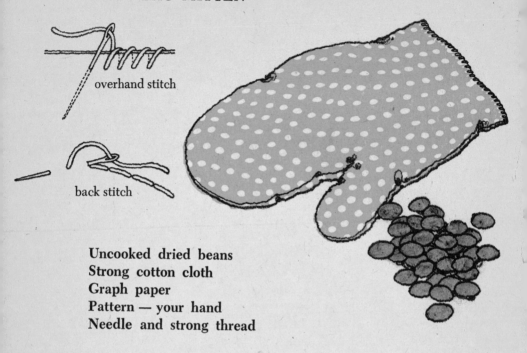

overhand stitch

back stitch

Uncooked dried beans
Strong cotton cloth
Graph paper
Pattern — your hand
Needle and strong thread

1. Place your hand on the graph paper with fingers closed and thumb apart. Trace your hand in pencil and round out the outline to make the mitten.

2. Now cut out your penciled pattern, pin it to a piece of cloth folded double, and cut out your cloth mitten. Use a back stitch to sew together all edges but the wrist-opening. (Sew with "wrong" side out.)

3. Now turn the mitten inside out, stuff *loosely* with beans, turn in wrist edges, and sew together with small overhand stitches.

NOTE: You can also make other pattern shapes — maybe a round "Funny-Face" bean bag, using bright yarn or paint to make the face.

DOORSTOP

Brick
Felt or other heavy material
Scissors
White glue
Enamel house paint

1. Wash the brick clean and allow it to dry overnight.

2. Cut out a piece of felt to fit one side. Glue it on. (This felt side will keep your doorstop from scratching floors.)

3. Now paint the rest of the brick either white or a color, and let it dry thoroughly. You may need to give it two coats.

4. You can decorate the brick by painting fancy initials or a gay design on it.

FRUIT PLATTER

Dinner-sized (white) paper plates (3)
Crayons
Poster paints (opaque)
Glue
Plastic spray
Liquid wax

1. Glue the 3 plates together, one on top of the other. Place a weight in the center of the stack to hold it together while drying.

2. When dry, color a design or pattern on the top plate with crayons. Press down heavily with your crayons, but leave some areas of the plate white.

3. Paint the white areas of the top plate with an opaque water paint. It will not stick to the crayoned design.

4. Let the paint dry, then spray the whole platter with plastic spray. Repeat when first coat is dry.

5. When thoroughly dry, wax lightly. This will give you a surface that can be wiped clean with a damp cloth. Now you have a platter strong enough to hold fruit or to carry drinking glasses.

NOTEPAPER SPECIALS

Plain white notepaper (with envelopes)
Pressed and dried flowers, leaves, grass
Clear (colorless) nail polish

1. Arrange your flowers or other materials on a practice piece of paper. Keep your arrangement simple and not lumpy. Remember, it will be crushed down when placed in an envelope.

2. When you are ready to transfer your arrangement to the notepaper, spread the nail polish on the front of a folded note in the area where your design is to be. Then, *quickly* place the flowers on that area, tapping them down so that they are flat.

3. Now, *carefully* brush over your arrangement with the nail polish, stroking outward from the centers of your material. Keep your notes separate to dry *thoroughly* before using or putting away.

NOTE: You can make up a set of 6 notes and package them in a plastic bag to sell.

PINE CONE ORNAMENTS

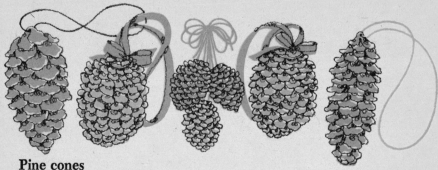

Pine cones
Red, green, or white spray paint
Gold or silver paint
String or thread
Paint brush

1. Put the pine cones on a sheet of newspaper — to protect surfaces from spray. You can also fold a piece of cardboard to make a two-panel, prop-up screen to place behind the cones.

2. Spray the cones on one side. Allow them to dry, then spray the other side.

3. When the cones are dry, paint the tips in gold or silver and let dry.

4. If cones are "soft," sew a foot-long heavy thread through the bottom of each cone. If they are wooden-like, tie ribbon through the bottom spurs of each cone. Now, you have glistening ornaments for packages, a wreath, a Christmas tree, or to hang on a door with a big bow.

PENCIL HOLDER

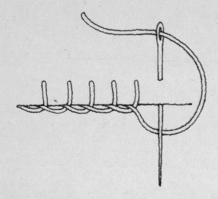

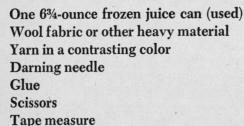

One 6¾-ounce frozen juice can (used)
Wool fabric or other heavy material
Yarn in a contrasting color
Darning needle
Glue
Scissors
Tape measure

1. Wash the juice can well, and dry.

2. Measure the height and the distance around the can and use these measurements to cut out a piece of wool material to fit the can, allowing an extra ½ inch for overlap.

3. Using yarn, sew a blanket stitch along the top and bottom edges of your material. You can also embroider a flower design in the center of it.

4. Now smear the can with glue and press the piece of material firmly around the juice can (*see page 20*). The stitched borders should be at the top and bottom of your pencil holder. Let dry and use.

Cardboard egg carton
Soil
Package of flower seeds, such as marigolds

NOTE: This item will give you a good head start on a spring garden. It's one way to begin your garden before the weather is warm enough for planting seeds outdoors.

1. Remove the top half of the egg carton. Be sure the bottom half is clean. Then spoon ½ inch of soil into each cup of the bottom half.

2. Carefully shake the seeds from the package into a dish, and sprinkle two or three into each cup. Cover lightly with ¼ to ½ inch more soil. Sprinkle water in each cup so that soil is moist. Do *not* flood.

3. Place your garden starter in a sunny spot near a window. Sprinkle water on it each day. In about a week, tiny pale green leaves will begin to poke through the soil. When the weather is warm enough and the plants are several inches high, you can move your garden outdoors.

4. To do this, cut your garden starter lengthwise, so you have two sections of six cups each. Now, "plant" the sections in the ground. The cardboard will slowly break up in the soil and, with care, your plants will continue to grow in neat little rows.

NOTE: If you do not have a cardboard egg carton, you can plant in a plastic (styrofoam) carton, and lift seedlings out carefully with a spoon when transplanting to soil outdoors.

PICTURE-PRETTY COASTERS

Piece of cardboard, 8 by 12 inches
Old magazines
Glue
Ruler
Sharp scissors
Clear shellac (thinned)
Liquid wax

1. Measure out 6 squares, 4 inches square, on your cardboard. Cut out the squares.

2. Tear out colorful pictures from magazines, and cut up these pictures into sizes and shapes to cover both sides of the cardboard squares. Make the magazine cutouts overlap so that no cardboard is showing. Or you might use just one large picture for each side of a square. Be sure your pasting job is smooth and there are no rough edges or bumpy spots on your coasters.

3. When the glue is dry, give each coaster two coats of thinned shellac. (Allow it to dry between coats.) When the second coat has dried, rub with wax. Your coasters are now waterproof and ready for use.

NOTE: If you prefer, you can make round coasters. Use the rim of a large glass to trace circles on the cardboard, which you can cut out and cover.

NAPKIN RINGS

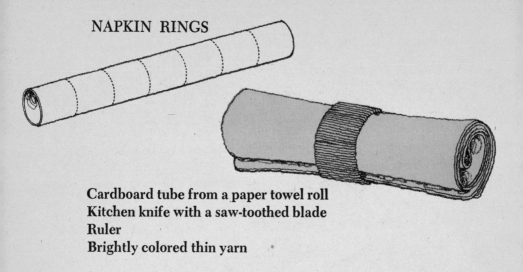

Cardboard tube from a paper towel roll
Kitchen knife with a saw-toothed blade
Ruler
Brightly colored thin yarn

1. On the paper towel tube mark off 4 or 5 sections for napkin rings. (Each should be from 1½ to 2 inches wide.)

2. Place the tube on a kitchen bread board or other cutting surface. Hold the tube down gently but firmly with one hand and with the other *very carefully* "saw" the sections apart with the tooth-edged knife. Now you have the "ring" for each napkin holder.

3. Take one end of a piece of yarn. Hold it against the side of the ring, then wrap the rest of the yarn around the ring until all the cardboard is covered. Fasten the end of the yarn by tying it on the inside of the ring. Now all your napkin rings need are napkins!

NOTE: You can also paint your rings inside and out with enamel paint instead of winding them with yarn. Let them dry overnight, then paint on initials.

SNACK-BIRD HOLDER

Aluminum kitchen foil (lightweight 12-inch roll)
Paper or styrofoam cup

1. Cut down cup until it measures 2 inches high.

2. Rip off a piece of foil about 18–20 inches long, and place the cup about 6–8 inches from right end of your foil.

3. Now, crush the foil up, around, and in the cup so that cup is completely covered inside and out. At the right end, make a small head, gently pulling the front part into a beak, and the top part into a crest.

4. Now fan out the left end of the foil into a tail. You can make feathers by making cuts into the tail.

NOTE: If your bird isn't steady enough to stay up by itself, don't worry. Candy or peanuts will keep it steady when you fill the cup.

TREASURE BOX

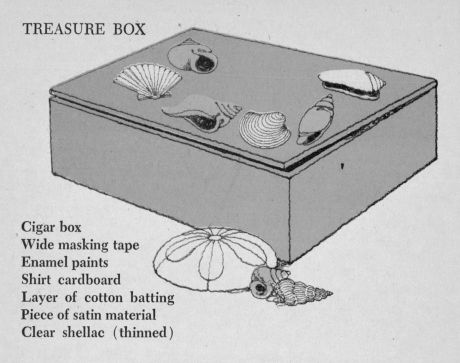

Cigar box
Wide masking tape
Enamel paints
Shirt cardboard
Layer of cotton batting
Piece of satin material
Clear shellac (thinned)

1. Put on a strip of masking tape where cover is attached to box.

2. Shellac top and sides of box and let dry thoroughly.

3. Next, paint top and sides of box, using bright enamel paint, and let it dry.

4. Now you can decorate the box with contrasting enamel paint in designs to suit your treasures (shells, butterflies, rocks).

5. To make a jewelry box, glue fancy paper on inside cover and make a jewelry "pillow": Cut down a shirt cardboard to fit box bottom easily; place a layer of cotton batting on it, and cover with larger piece of satin, which you glue tightly to under sides. Insert in box.

BOOK MARKS

Hair clip
Felt or finely woven cloth
Scissors
White glue
Straight pins
Paper

1. First, draw an outline design about 2 inches long on paper and cut it out to use for a pattern. Pin it on a piece of felt and cut — or pin it to a folded piece of cloth and cut out twin designs.

2. Glue the felt design to one side of the hair clip. If you have twin designs, glue cloth twin to each side of hair clip, and sew edges with small blanket stitch (*see page 27*).

3. You can also make strip book marks out of felt, leather or plastic leather. The strip can be 1½ by 6 inches. Decorate the felt with paints or a yarn design; cut a fringe at one end of leather strip.

CHRISTMAS TREE PRETTIES

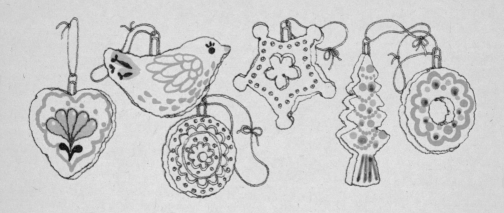

4 cups flour
1 cup salt
1½ cups water
Paper clips
Tempera paints
Thread
Clear plastic spray

NOTE: As this involves using the oven, have an adult light it and set it for 350°.

1. Mix the flour, salt, and water to make a flour clay. Rub your hands with flour and knead the mixture for at least five minutes. At first the clay will be thin and sticky. Keep working it with your hands — it will thicken.

2. Next, mold the clay. You can shape Christmas wreaths, trees, stars, or whatever strikes your fancy. For adding details, try using a toothpick to "etch" the clay. Finished pieces should be no thicker than ½ inch and no bigger than 3 inches.

3. Stick one end of a paper clip into each shape for a hanging hook.

4. Cover a cookie sheet with foil and place your clay shapes on it. Bake in an oven at 350° for about 12–20 minutes. When done, your clay will be light brown in color. When tapped with a fork, it will make a solid ringing sound.

5. Decorate your clay ornaments with paints. When paint is dry, spray ornaments with clear plastic coating. Tie a thread through each paper clip and trim a merry tree for the holidays.

5-inch by 7-inch index cards
Rubber cement or glue
Felt or other material
Scissors
Felt-tip pen

1. Make several sketches of simple designs you can cut out of fabric. Flowers, birds, Christmas trees, animals, butterflies, and fruit are some ideas. If you like, you can paint sky or grass as a background, or make a line-design with a colored felt pen.

2. Make a paper pattern of the design you choose. Pin this pattern to the fabric, or you can hold it to the fabric and make a pencil outline.

3. Cut the fabric. If you have used pins, remove them.

4. Now glue your design-in-fabric on the *unlined* side of the index card. Use only *small* amounts of glue. Otherwise it will soak through the material. For a fancier design, you can use several different materials on a card, but keep the surface smooth and flat. Remember, it must go through the mails.

5. On the lined side of the index card, make a dividing line in pen. The left-hand side is for your message, the right-hand side is for the ·address. The stamp should go in the upper right-hand corner.

39

CLOTHESPIN MEMO HOLDER

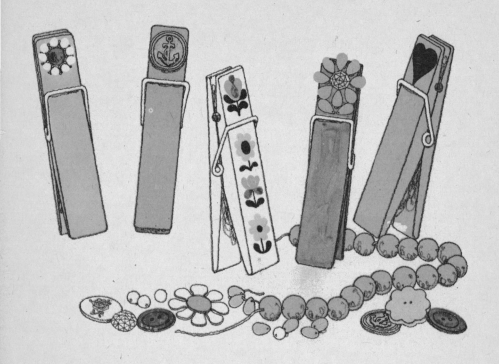

Wooden clip clothespin (one with a wire spring)
Enamel paint
Fancy buttons or beads from old jewelry

1. Paint the wooden part of the clothespin, inside the "wings" as well as outside, and let it dry.

2. Glue buttons or beads on the small clip part. Or, if you prefer, paint on a design. You now have a handy — and handsome — memo holder for someone's desk.

SPONGE TOYS

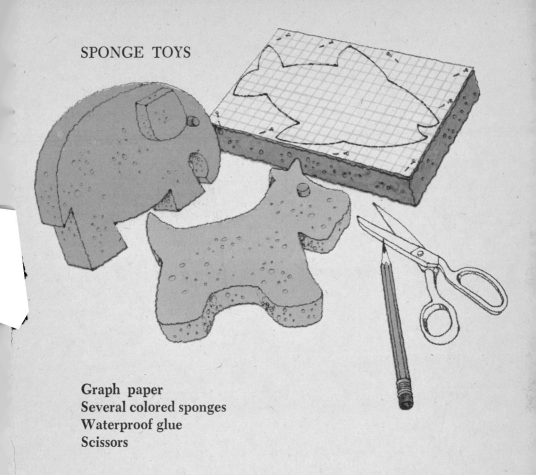

Graph paper
Several colored sponges
Waterproof glue
Scissors

1. Trace outline of the sponge onto graph paper.

2. Now draw a pattern shown here (or make your own design) and transfer it to the sponge shape you've drawn on the graph paper.

3. Cut out the shape, pin it onto the sponge, and cut out your sponge animal with sharp scissors.

4. Use the scraps from each sponge to make eyes, noses, mouths, etc., on the other animals. Glue these features on. Result: soft, waterproof toys for young children.

PAD FOR HOT PLATES

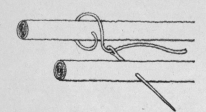

Old magazines
Glue
Long thin knitting needle
Sharp sewing needle
Thread
Scissors

1. To make a 6-inch square hot plate you will need to roll up about 25 colorful, shiny magazine pages. Tear them out carefully.

2. Starting at one corner, roll each page diagonally — and tightly — around the knitting needle. Touch the end corner with glue to hold it and remove the knitting needle. You should have a tube about the size of a fat straw.

3. When all 25 are made lay them side by side and sew through each one about 2 inches on either side of the middle.

4. Trim each end so that you have an even square.

NOTE: If you don't want to sew them, you can glue them side by side onto a sheet of thin cardboard and trim down to a 6-inch square.

TIE RACK

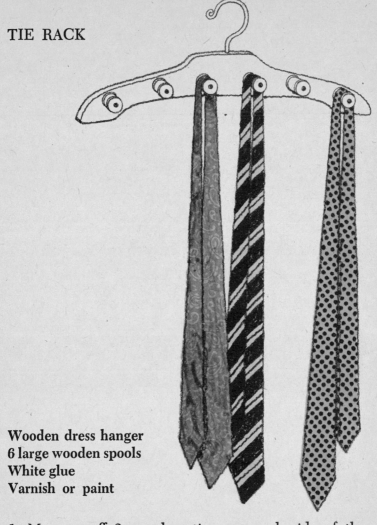

Wooden dress hanger
6 large wooden spools
White glue
Varnish or paint

1. Measure off 3 equal sections on each side of the hanger and mark them with a pencil dot.

2. Glue one flat side of each spool at each dot. Let dry for several hours.

3. Paint or varnish your tie rack, and hang up in free space — on the shower curtain rod, for example — to dry.

OTTO-THE-OCTOPUS DISH

9 paper cupcake holders
8 popsicle sticks
Cardboard
Glue
Crayons
Scissors

1. Turn one cup upside down over the bottom of a glass, and draw a funny face for Otto, using your crayons.

2. Then, using the glass as a guide, trace a circle on the cardboard and cut it out.

3. Arrange the popsicle sticks around the circle as if they were spokes in a wheel. Glue the stick ends to the cardboard circle.

4. Turn over the cardboard circle and glue it to the edges of your Otto-the-Octopus cup. Glue bottoms of remaining 8 cups to the ends of the 8 sticks. When dry, fill the cups with goodies. Your Otto-the-Octopus dish is complete!

PEANUT NECKLACE

Peanuts in the shells
Gold spray paint
or cans of quick-dry enamel
Needle
Thread

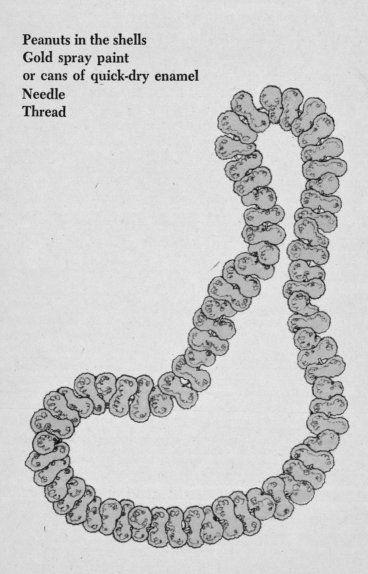

1. Cut off a length of strong thread about 4 inches longer than you wish your finished necklace to be. Put one end of the thread through the eye of the finest needle that you can thread and tie a knot at the other end.

2. Now push the needle through each peanut. When all the peanuts are strung, pull off the needle and tie the thread ends together.

3. To spray your necklace with paint, place it on newspapers or cardboard, and prop a cardboard screen in back to keep spray from drifting. Let top side dry, then turn necklace and spray the other side.

4. Instead of spraying, you can decorate the peanuts with stripes or designs, using brightly colored enamel paint and a brush. Do this *before* you string the peanuts.

IMPORTANT WARNING: Do *not* eat the peanuts after they are painted or sprayed!

PIN CUSHION

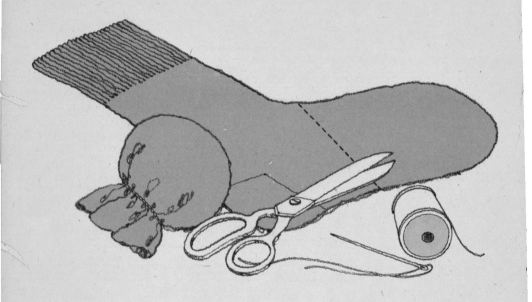

An old sock
Shavings from sharpened pencils, or sawdust
Needle
Thread
Scissors
Medium-sized hand-cream jar
Enamel paint
Cloth

1. Soak off the jar label and clean the jar well. Let it dry. Decorate the outside with your paints and let dry.

2. Cut across the sock about 4 inches above the toe end. Stuff this toe with the pencil shavings and sew up the open end as shown (to make it rounder).

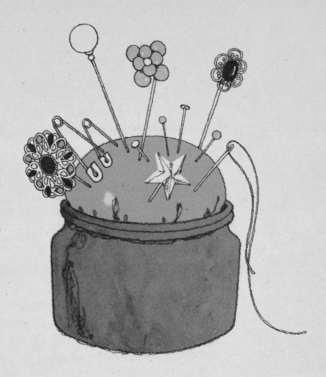

3. Push the stuffed sock into the jar, toe end up. Stick in your pins and needles. You'll find the pencil shavings will keep them rust-free.

4. For a more elegant-looking pin cushion, you can cover the toe part with velvet or a cotton print that goes with your room.

5. To make a "cover," use your sock-toe (flat) as a pattern before you stuff it. Place the (flat) sock-toe on the folded cover fabric. Cut the fabric a seam's width bigger than the sock, and stitch on the wrong side.

6. Now turn your cover right side out, stuff the sock-toe and pull the cover tightly over it. Stitch bottom edge to sock and insert in jar.

BIRD FEEDER

Styrofoam or plastic tray from supermarket package
String, 4 pieces each about 20 inches long
Peanut butter
Cereal

1. Clean the tray. Punch 4 small holes ⸏ ıt, one in each corner. Knot each string ə⸍ ɔne end, draw through each hole, then tie tʰ⸍ 4 ends together so your feeder will hang.

2. Spread globs of peɑ ɑt butter on the tray. Sprinkle cereal, such ɐ ɔatmeal, on top. Hang your feeder on a tree ꞵᵣanch to treat your feathered friends.

HANDY HOOKS

Pull-back tops from soda cans
Small magnets
Felt
Scissors
Glue

1. Cut out a small fruit or animal shape from the felt. Glue this on the ring part of the pull-back top. Then bend the tab end of the top to form a hook.

2. Glue a magnet on the back of the ring. Stick it onto a stove or refrigerator door. Your hook is ready for potholders.

PLASTIC LOOP BELT

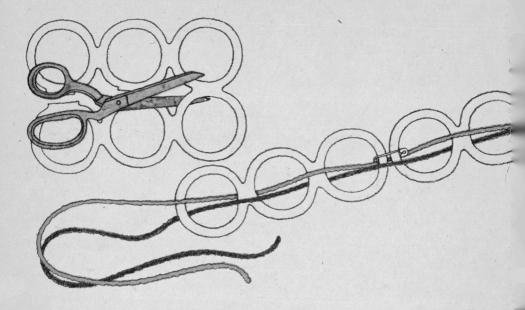

Plastic holders from six-pack soda cans
Heavy (bulky) yarn
Scissors
Safety pins

1. Cut each plastic holder-set carefully in half, length-wise, so that you have four to six 3-loop holders. Lay them out in a single row. Connect them with medium-small safety pins.

2. Hold the loops around your waist for size. (You'll probably need three 3-loop soda or four 3-loop juice holders for yourself.) If the belt is too large, cut off some loops. Allow about an inch of space between the two end loops.

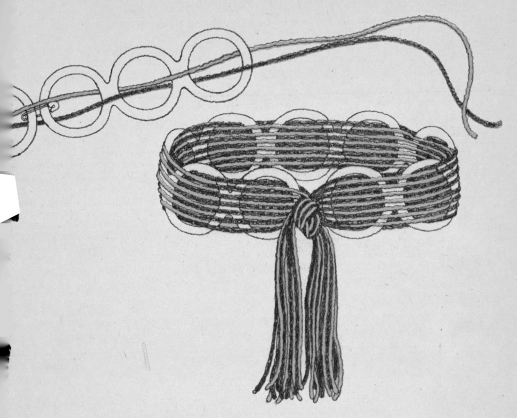

3. Now, thread a piece of yarn through the loops —
   under one, over the next, and so on. Leave about
   10 inches of yarn hanging at each end. Weave
   through another piece of yarn, this time reversing
   your over-under pattern. Keep weaving through
   yarn, and alternating rows, until the space in the
   loops is filled up. Remember to leave enough yarn
   hanging at each end.

4. When your weaving is done, remove the safety pins.
   Try on your belt. Tie the hanging yarn ends in a
   loose knot at the front.

HANDY DANDY JAR HOLDERS

Baby food jars (6)
Wooden board 15 inches long
Nails
Hammer
Varnish

1. Varnish the piece of wood. Allow it to dry.

2. Wash the jars and their caps thoroughly, and dry. Arrange the caps on a piece of wood. Make sure the *top* side of each cap is against the wood. Nail the caps to the wood. Now screw the jars onto the caps.

3. You have a fine holder that Dad can fasten under the shelf above his work bench. The screw-on jars are great for storing nails and other small items.

PRICKLY VASE

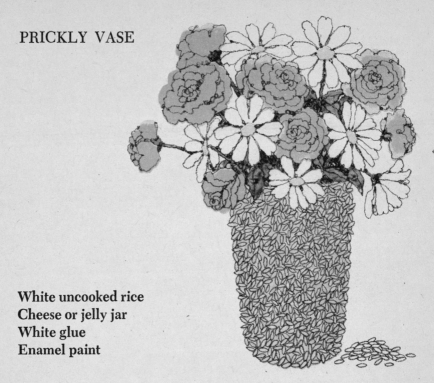

White uncooked rice
Cheese or jelly jar
White glue
Enamel paint

1. Wash and dry your glass thoroughly.

2. Apply glue to outside of glass, all around.

3. Sprinkle some rice on wax paper, and roll the gluey glass in the rice. Let it dry. If your rice coating seems too thin, add more glue (with a brush) and sprinkle on more rice.

4. Decorate your prickly vase by dabbing on paint. For a multi-color effect leave some of the rice unpainted. When it is dry, fill your vase with water and flowers.

CAUTION: For best cleaning results, wash vase only on the inside and with a cloth. *Don't submerge in water.*

SOAP DISH

Large clam shell
Gold paint
Plastic sandwich bag
Ribbon

1. Clean the shell carefully and paint the "ledge" or "hinge" part in gold. You might also paint stripes or another design, using oil paint, on the inside of the shell.

2. When dry, package your shell in a plastic bag tied with a ribbon. You now have a soap dish pretty enough to give as a gift or sell to a neighbor.

BATHROOM CUP HOLDER

Pint cream or milk container
Old terry cloth towel
Glue
Scissors
Hole puncher

1. Wash out the container and cut off the top. Cut three sides so that they measure 2 inches from the bottom. Leave the fourth side its original height.

2. Measure one piece of terry towel to fit the three sides, one for the fourth side, and one to cover the bottom of your container. Cut them out. Glue the terry cloth on the outside of the three short sides and the bottom. Glue the long piece on the *inside* of the tall side of the container. Let the glue dry.

3. Now, using a hole puncher, make a hole near the top center of the tall side. The cup holder can be hung from a picture hook driven into the wall. (Be sure to let your mom or dad do that!)

CANDLE TREE

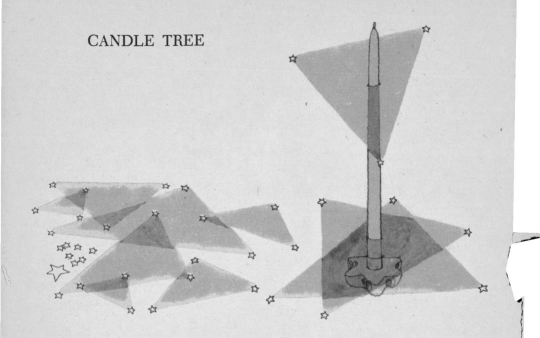

Green 10-inch (slender) candle in individual holder
Green net material
Box of tiny sticker stars
One large sticker star
Scissors

1. Cut out about 10 different sized triangles from the green net. The largest might have 8-inch sides; the smallest, 2-inch sides. Cut a small slit in the center of each triangle. Paste the stars on the tips of the triangles.

2. Next, slip the largest triangle, star side up, over the candle, push it to the bottom. Slip the next largest triangle over the candle. Push it down to about an inch above the first triangle. Turn the second triangle so that it points in different directions from the first.

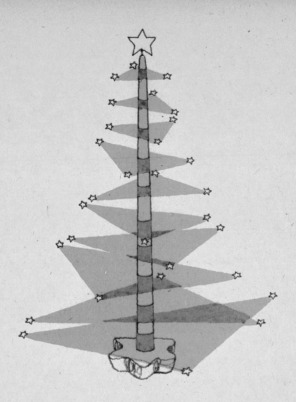

3. Keep repeating this until all your triangles are on the candle. Paste the large sticker star on the wick of the candle.

IMPORTANT WARNING: The candle tree is *not* fireproof and should *not* be lit. Use it only as a holiday ornament or centerpiece.

WASTEBASKET

Old wastebasket or one-gallon ice-cream container
Contact paper
Scissors

1. Thoroughly clean and dry the ice-cream container or wastebasket.

2. Measure the height and distance around. Measure and cut out a piece of contact paper to fit, allowing a ½-inch overlap. Press it carefully around the outside of your container.

3. You can also glue on pictures from magazines so that they overlap and cover the surface. If you're a baseball fan, cut out pictures of your favorite players and glue them on in a *montage* (a mixed-up, overlapping arrangement). Other themes might be horses, dancers, TV stars, or pop singers.

4. If you use this method, it's a good idea to apply a coat of thin shellac to protect your pictures.

5. Still another idea is to glue on material that matches your drapes or spread. You'll want to shellac this, also.

BOOK RACK

One 2-pound round oatmeal or corn meal box
Flat piece of wood 1 foot long and 4 inches wide
Scissors or a saw-toothed knife
Contact paper
White glue

1. Make sure the box is clean. Then glue on the lid tightly. Mark and "saw" out with the knife a section of the box as shown.

2. Cover edges and outside of box with gay contact paper.

3. Glue the back the long way onto the wood for a firm base. Your books will fit in as shown.

GARDEN HELPER

Soft drink bottle-carrier
Enamel paint

This is an easy-to-make, handy-to-have item. It's useful for garden tools, small household cleaning tools, or a handyman's tools. All you do is paint the bottle carrier with bright enamel and decorate it to suit its use. A handy gift or a helper for you.

PLACEMAT

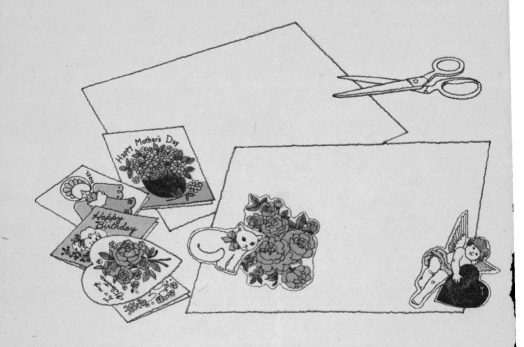

Old greeting cards
Clear contact paper
Scissors

1. Cut two pieces of the clear contact paper into rectangles, 15 inches by 11 inches. Don't remove backing. Lay one down flat on your work space.

2. Now cut out pictures or designs from the greeting cards. Arrange them face up on the contact paper. Work with them until you have your arrangement the way you want it.

3. Remove the backing from the *other* piece of contact paper, and lay it, sticky side up, next to your arrangement.

4. Now move your cards, one by one, still face up, to the sticky contact paper. Press them into place firmly so they stick.

5. When your entire arrangement is transferred, strip the other piece of contact paper and place it very carefully on top of your cards. Press smoothly. Trim if necessary. Now you have a colorful placemat with a plastic surface that can be wiped easily. Happy eating!

PART II
THINGS TO DO

SCRAP ACTION

Old newspapers, empty cans, and glass bottles can be recycled (used again). By saving them for recycling, people help cut down on litter and on wasting valuable resources. But no one wants the garage piled with old scrap. Many people don't have the time to take their scrap to recycling centers. So you might offer *your* services.

First check to see who in your community buys scrap for recycling. It may be a bottling plant, a metal or paper company, or even your local government. Find out where and when to bring the scrap, and what prices are paid for it.

You'll also want to find out *how* the scrap should be delivered. For instance, some companies want newspapers tied in bundles. Or they might request that bottles be cleaned and labels removed. The better finding-out job you do at this stage, the easier your job will be later on.

Next, let people know you are available. Tell them what time on what day you make pick-ups. You will probably want to make pick-ups either on the same day, or perhaps the day before you deliver scrap to the recycling center. If you are charging people for this service, tell them what your fee is.

On pick-up day, you will want to have the right tools . . . rope for tying up newspapers, perhaps a wagon for carrying your scrap, gloves for handling glass and cans.

Many places ask that all cans be crushed. This can be done by removing the label and both lids. (Sometimes the labels have to be soaked off.) Then, stomp on the can *sideways,* on the sidewalk or garage floor. Slip both lids into the crushed can.

On delivery day, check again to make sure you have met all the requirements for selling scrap. Then, step right up with your scrap heap haul.

NUMBER, PLEASE

Here's an idea you can apply in several ways. Become a number painter.

You will need to invest in a stencil with the numbers 0 to 9 on it, some outdoor paint and a narrow brush. Now, visit your neighbors to see if the numbers on their doors, mailboxes, or curbs need freshening up. (If you paint on curbs, be sure to get permission from your city or town, if needed.) With your stencil, you can paint neat, easy-to-read numbers, a real aid to mailmen and visitors.

Before setting out on this project, it's a good idea to practice a bit, so you learn to avoid dripping paint or smudging numbers.

STORYTELLER

Are there lots of little children in your neighborhood? Do you have younger brothers and sisters who aren't old enough to go to school? Why not set up a storytelling hour? Boys and girls who cannot yet read, love being read to.

Look through some of your favorite storybooks. Select a few short, easy-to-read tales you think a younger child would enjoy reading too. Try to choose stories with lots of sound effects so you can keep your listener's attention.

Find a quiet, comfortable place where you can read in peace.

At first read to just one child at a time. After you become more experienced, you might read to two or three children. You'll probably find that your listeners have favorite stories and will make "special requests" for you to read them. If you are reading to a group, be sure to give each child a chance to make his request.

And, of course, if you are charging for your story hours, talk to the child's parents first. Many will enjoy the free time you make possible for them by reading to their little ones.

ERRANDS UNLIMITED

Set up an errand service. You can get lots of free practice right in your own home! Does Mom want you to buy milk at the corner store or borrow sugar from a neighbor or mail some letters? Try following these steps as you go about your errands:

1. Be prepared. Listen *carefully* to instructions. Make sure you understand them.
2. Be prompt. Complete the errand as quickly as possible.
3. Be resourceful. If you run into any snags, ask for further instructions — and use your head. For instance, if your mother sends you for milk and the store is closed, that's a snag. If there were another store nearby, you might go there. If not, call her or go back for more instructions.
4. Be cheerful and polite. People like a helper who seems to enjoy his work.

Once you've passed these steps with flying colors at home, you might offer your services to nearby friends and neighbors. Let people know you are on call for errands. Tell them how much you charge and the kinds of things you can do. One idea is to make little calling cards with your name and telephone number on them. That way people have a handy reference when an errand needs doing.

YARD JOBS

For every season, there's a yard job to be done. If you enjoy being outdoors, perhaps you'll like these projects. Most of them require lots of energy, so perhaps you'll need a partner.

Fall — Rake leaves. You'll need a lightweight yard rake so you don't uproot grass. Rake the leaves into piles. Find out from your employer what he wants done with them (carted away, piled for compost, etc.).

Winter — Shovel snow. Use a wide, flat, light metal snow shovel for shoveling sidewalks or patios. Clear all steps thoroughly so no icy patches form.

Spring — Clear gardens of leaves and dead stalks, being careful not to injure new plants. Have a basket or plastic yard bag to put in stuff to be carried away.

Summer — Keep a yard tidy. Pick up any litter, fallen branches, grass cuttings, and scattered stones. Make sure items such as trash cans are in their proper place. Sweep sidewalks. Sprinkle lawns and water gardens.

BE A SALESMAN

You might sell some things you made yourself (*see the* "Things to Make" *section*), or some things you have assembled. For instance, put together a travel snack kit. You might include gum, a packet of peanut butter crackers, and some hard candy. Package your kit in a plastic sandwich bag, tie with a ribbon, then add a label — Go Anywhere Snack Kit.

Perhaps you can try other kinds of goody kits as well — holidays, TV snacks, etc.

If you're buying the ingredients for your kits, keep a record of the cost. Decide how many kits you can make and how much they will sell for. Figure out how many kits you must sell before you make a profit.

NOTE: When selling things, it's a good idea to start out with some change in case people don't have the exact amount.

CLEAN CLOSET SALE

This project has two purposes — a tidy closet, and some spending money.

First clean out your closet — and any other places where you stash old toys, books, and games. Decide which things you no longer need or want, and whether you want to sell or swap them.

Check with your parents before putting anything up for sale or swap. Then set up a table or bench outside for your sale. Display your wares. You may want to make price tags and a big sign — Sale Today!

Keep a record of what you sell and how much you get for it. Keep your money in a box or other safe place.

THIS CAN BELONGS TO _____

Where garbage or trash cans are used, lids often get lost or mixed up on "collection day." You might perform a needed service by painting names and street numbers on garbage can lids.

Use a one-inch brush and some brightly colored house paint. Print your letters in clear strokes. If your writing isn't too readable, use a stencil to form your letters. Some people might want their name on the side of the can too. If you're getting paid for this service, you might charge by the letter.

WAKE-UP SERVICE

You can do what the desk clerk does in a hotel. Offer to call people at a certain time each morning so that they can get up on time. But be sure to ask your parents' permission to use the telephone in this way.

This is a good job only for regular early risers, not sleepy-heads!

GET DOWN TO BUSINESS

You've decided to earn some extra money. Your parents have given their okay. The next question is: *What will you make or do?*

Think about where you live. What are some items or services that would do well in your neighborhood? What would people in your apartment building need? What would neighbors down the block like? What groups do you belong to that might use your services?

Decide what you do well — and enjoy doing. If you're not sure, try out a few things.

Consider your time and materials. When are you available to work? How much time are you willing to spend on this project? What tools does your family already own? What scrap materials can you easily find?

Once you've decided on what you will do, think about how you will go about it.

To keep track of your time and know what materials cost, make a sample of anything you want to sell. Show it to people to find out if they want it and how much you should charge. Then take orders so that you'll know how many items to make. Set up an assembly line. If you're making 10 identical items, complete the first step on *each* before going on to the next step. That way you can save some time and materials.

Advertise your services or wares. Send out cards, ring doorbells, or put up signs.

Have references ready — for people who don't know you. Have the names of one or two adults who do know you, and will speak for your reliability, etc. Of course, if you use someone's name as a reference, be sure you have his permission.

Don't expect your parents to finish what *you* start. This is *your* business — and your responsibility. If you are going to be late on a job or on finishing a project, call and explain *ahead of time*. If you don't want to continue in a job, tell people ahead of time. If you make a mistake, apologize. If you break or damage something, offer to pay for it.

What else does a businessman or woman need to do?

Find out how much materials cost. If you need to buy anything for your project, check on prices first.

Find out where and how you can get the best buy. If you spend a lot of money, you'll have to sell that many more items to make your money back.

Decide what to charge. What is the going rate for similar jobs in your area? How much do you need to charge for items in order to make money? How much will your customers be willing to pay?

Keep records of how much you spend on materials, and how much you earn from sales. Keep notes on who orders what and when it's promised. Does anyone owe you money? Keep a record of that! Keep a record of your time too. Another way records can help: If, in a few months time, you decide to start another business project, you'll already have a list of good customers.

Make schedules. Suppose you've got a lot of orders for Christmas gifts. Figure out how long each thing takes to make, spread your work over a period of time, and set deadlines for yourself.

Send out (or deliver) bills. If people don't pay you right away, give them a bill. It's an accurate and easy way to remind them. Bills should include the date, your name and address, the work or item sold, and the price.

Give receipts. When people pay you, give them a receipt. This should say PAID, and indicate the amount.

Say "thank-you" when you make a sale — and when you don't. Being polite always helps to make and keep friends — and customers.

Have a good time being busy your way.

TIPS FOR USING GLUES AND PAINTS

GLUE — Spread smoothly and not too thickly. Wipe away any extra glue with a rag. Allow time for the glue to dry, so that it will hold permanently.

KINDS OF GLUE: *Rubber cement* is good for joining paper, cardboard, and rubber. *Resin glue* will join plastic foam as well as paper, cloth, leather, or wood. *White glue* is good for joining heavier materials such as wood, glass, leather, plastics, china, fabrics, foil, and also paper. *Epoxy cement* joins metal and cement as well as other materials. For some paper projects you can use a paste that you can make by mixing flour and water.

PAINTS AND PAINTING SUPPLIES — *Always be sure to read the directions carefully on any paint supplies before using.* Use in well-ventilated place NOT near open fire. Cover work surfaces with newspapers.

For storing paint supplies, arrange with your family for the shelf space you'll need. Jars or cans of paint should not be stored in your boodle box. Also, have plenty of clean-up rags on hand for wiping up. After using paint rags, throw them away.

Some of the painting supplies you might use in your projects are:

Transparent watercolors — These come in tablets or tubes, and work best on paper. Colors should be mixed with water before applying.

Opaque water paints — These include the poster paints you may sometimes use in school. They come in jars of liquid or in powder form, and are mixed with water.

Novelty enamel paints — These are available in small, inexpensive jars and work well on many surfaces (glass, shells, rocks, wood). For cleaning brushes or thinning this paint, you'll need to use turpentine.

Oil-base house paints — These dry slowly. They come in cans of many sizes. There are flat (dull) paints for walls, and enamel for furniture or woodwork. If you are using paint from a large can, first stir it with a stick, then have an adult pour some into a small, clean, dry can or jar. Thin oil paints with turpentine or paint thinner. And use either one to clean brushes, wipe up spatters, etc.

CAUTION: Use spray paints outdoors if possible; put newspapers or cardboard behind object for a screen. Don't use on styrofoam. It will melt!

Latex house paints — These usually come in larger cans for household use. Fresh spatters, brushes, and hands can be cleaned with warm water. Latex paints dry in a few hours.

Shellac — Shellac is also put on with a brush. Be sure the surface you shellac is dry and *clean*. Before u_ing shellac it is best to thin it with a little denatured alc hol. (You can also use the denatured alcohol to clea your brush when you are through.) Shellac dries quic

Va h is really clear oil paint. Make sure the surface y re going to work on is clean, dry, and not greasy. v varnish with a brush. It will dry faster if you t with a little turpentine. Use turpentine to clean your brush and hands.

NOTE: If you need to buy small quantities of house paints, you will probably find that your local paint store has the best selection.